DOG MAN

~~the~~ Behind the Scenes

One Time, George met Harold in kindergarten.

nice to meet you.

me too.

They became best friends and started making comics.

Their very First comic was a epic Novella called:

The ADVENCHERS of DOG Man

AKShin

LAFFS

LAUGHS

by George and Harold

Over the years, they made **TONS** OF DOG MAN comic Books.

DOG MAN & FLIPPY

DOG MAN in SPACE

Then one day in 4th Grade, They got a new idea.

They started making a new Comic.

Captain Underpants

By George and Harold

soon, their lives got **REALLY** Complicated!

There was Danger...

...HORROR...

ZAP!

...and ridiculously convoluted plot lines.

And just when it seemed like things couldn't get any worse...

Things got better.

Hey!

?

All the drama had come to a end.

But there were still lots of unanswered questions.

Where are our doubles?

Where's Tony, Orlando, and Dawn?

George and Harold searched their tree house for clues...

...but soon, they got distracted.

Hey, Look!

aw, COOL!

It's a box full of ~~this~~ old Dog Man comics we made when we were kids.

Hey, I forgot all about these!!!

They read For hours

Ha Ha Ha Ha

I crack me up!

How about a Dog Man comic?

Ok!

And Together, the two friends wrote and drew and Laughed all afternoon.

George tried To SpeLL more better...

Dict-ion-ary

... Harold tried To draw more simpler...

... and Thus, **DOG Man** was reborn anewish!

class!

DOG MAN

Enjoy it!!!

DOG MAN

CHAPTER 1
A Hero is Unleashed

BY
George and Harold

HEY!

OFFicer Knight and Greg the dog...

...You got dirty shoes and Dog hair everywhere!

and Greg the dog is smart...

Thinky

but his body is his weakness!

Fleas
P.U.
can't drive car
can't punch

Yeah, but what if they work **TOGETHER???**

Hmmm...That might be a problem!

Fortunately, I've got a solution!

Bomb

Tee-hee!

Bomb

Officer Knight and Greg ran to defuse the bomb.

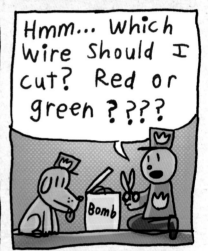

Hmm... Which wire should I cut? Red or green????

Grrr!

Ok! Green it is!!!!

And so...

SNIP

Soon the doctor came in with some supa sad news.

Boo-Hoo-Hoo!

I'm sorry, Greg, but your body is dying.

and your head is dying too, cop.

Rats! I sure hate my dying head!

But just when all seemed lost...

HEY!

→ nurse Lady

Why don't we sew Greg's head onto cop's body?

Good idea, nurse Lady! You're a genius!!!

Hooray!

So they had a big operation. The doctor cut off Greg's head and sewed it onto cop's body.

What a Lucky day!

And soon, a brand-new crime-fighting sensation ~~was~~ was unleashed.

HooRaY FoR DoG Man!

The news spread Quickly!

CiTY NEWS

Dog Man is World's greatest COP!!!!!

Rats!!! I unwittingly created the greatest cop of ever!!!!!

Fortunately, I know ~~where~~ JUST how to stop him!!

The next day...

CITY NEWS
DOG MAN Rules

chief

Well Well, Well!

So you're the world's most greatest cop, eh?

chief

Well you better watch your step around here, bub!

chief

I'm gonna keep my eye on you!

WeLL? What do you have To Say for yourself?

Lick

GET OUT OF HERE!

Poor Dog Man's Day had started out badly...

...but things were about to get worse!

Petey's secre Lab

24

But Dogs are **ALSO** afraid of...

VACUUM CLEANERS!

I built this baby Last night.

Gee, I Think firecrackers would have been easier.

Who asked You?

um... You did.

SLap

This has THOUSANDS OF dollars of the Latest TechnologY!!!

firecrackers only cost five bucks.

ENOUGH with the FirecRackers!

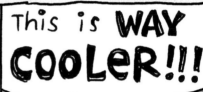

This is WAY COOLER!!!

And once I Turn it on...

OFF
ON

...it will chase DOG MAN...

...and it won't stop until he gets sucked up!!!

HAW HAW HAW

YEEE HAW!

ZOOOOM

PETEY'S SECRET LAB

Oh, DOG MAN...

27

This vacuum has a 6000 H.P. motor...

...an endless power supply...

...and the bag expands, so it can suck up almost anything!

When Dog Man heard the word "almost"...

...he got a good idea.

GULP!

Dude! That giant vacuum cleaner just swallowed my surfboard!

Bummer, dude.

SPLASH!

The vacuum followed Dog Man into the sea.

HEY! Let's get out of this water, OK? I can't swim!!!!

Besides---This vacuum cleaner isn't supposed to get wet!!!

No Fair!

Dog Man dived down...

So the vacuum started sucking up the sea.

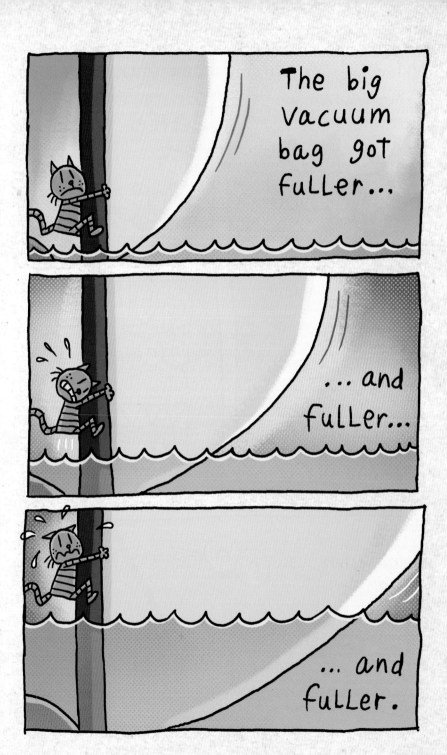

Meanwhile, under the water...

Dog Man was losing the battle.

GULP!

The vacuum cleaner had won the war.

or had he?

I gotta get out of here before this bag of sea water busts!

WHOA!

Boing

Boing

Petey grabbed on with his claws.

Suddenly, the vacuum bag began to rip.

Petey got washed away in the supa tidal wave.

It looked like this was the end...

39

O-RAMA

HERE'S HOW IT WORKS:

STEP 1.
First, place your left hand inside the dotted lines marked "Left hand here". Hold the book open FLAT!

STEP 2:
Grasp the right-hand page with your thumb and index finger (inside the dotted lines marked "Right Thumb Here").

STEP 3:
Now QUICKLY flip the right-hand page back and forth until the picture appears to be Animated.

(for extra fun, try adding your own sound-effects!)

The Tidal wave got smaller and smaller...

...until it ended at just the right spot.

HEY COPS!!! Dog man captured Peter!!

This calls for a celebration!!!

Remember, flip only page 43. Be sure you can see the picture on page 43 AND the one on page 45 while you flip.

Left hand here.

For he's a
JoLLy good
doggy!

Right
Thumb
here.

For he's a
JOLLY good
doggy!

Well, Dog Man, I guess I was wrong about you.

Put 'er there!!!

Lick

HOORAY FOR DOG MAN!

46

one day, this happened...

NO, DOG MAN!

NOOOOO!

STOP!

EVERYbodY! iN MY OFFICE **NOW!!!**

chief's office

ALRight, which one of You chewed up my tissues and ~~drank~~ ate my slippers and peed on my **F**loor?

Just as I Suspected!

Everybody **OUT**, except Dog Man!!

YOU...

ARE...

iN...

BiG...

54

UH, HOWDY, Mayor!

Don't "HOWDY Mayor" Me!

Have You Seen TODAY's news???

CITY NEWS
CHIEF is Soft on Crime

NEWS
Petey escapes From cat Jail 8 Times!

swipe

NEWS
Latest PoLL: EveryBody HaTes chief

swipe

56

Lick

Suddenly, Dog Man's Supa ears heard something.

...he rushed to the window...

Soon, my ~~red~~ evil plan will become reality.

Haw Haw Haw!

mayor

DOG MAN
FOLLOWED
Mayor
To a
Strange
Factory

ROBO-TIME
InDUSTRIES

He peeked
through a
window...

...and recorded
evidence on
his phone.

So, Dr. Scum... How is our evil
Robot coming Along?

Pretty good.

Awesome! Soon I shall use him to take over The city!

My evil plan will begin in 33 seconds!!!

Cool!

33 Seconds Later...

Cat Jail

Petey, you got a package.

Gimme it!

SSSSS

Awesome!!!

Now **I'm** completely invisible!

TOSS

Oh, Guard!!!

Yeah?

Uh-oh! Petey's Gone!!!

soon, Petey walked out of cat Jail.

Soon, the mayor returned to the police station.

KLUNK KLUNK KLU

I am ROBO CHIEF!

ROBO CHIEF is your new boss.

and **I** am ROBO CHIEF'S BOSS!

HAW HAW HAW HAW!!!

BZZZZ

Sorry, Dog Man. I got fired!

You must go on without me.

Pat Pat

Meanwhile...

Aah, it's good to be the King!

OK, DR. Scum, it's time to put our evil plan into action!!!

No Prob!

Soon, DR. Scum and his team of bad guys built a bunch of rotten businesses.

Tim's Burglar Supplies

Car Jack Lessons

Counter Fits

Fake Money

ILLegaL Stuff 4 SaLe

Stolen goods

Haw! Haw! Haw!

and all cops were ordered to stay away.

it was the perfect crime...

HAW! Haw! Haw!

...except for one thing!

HEY!

Look at all of those Rotten stores!

Hackers "Я" US

SUPA SCAM

Invisible Petey was not Happy!

⟨ ⟨ ⟩

Grrr!

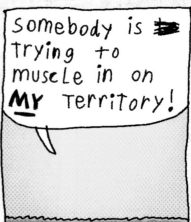

Somebody is ~~~~ trying to muscle in on **MY** Territory!

I have to Stop those evil jerks!

There can only be **ONE** villain in this town!!!

Invisible Petey got right to Work.

He Followed each customer into the rotten stores...

BiLL's Bombs

79

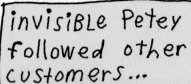
AAAAAAAAH! it's a Ghost!!!

BO!

invisible Petey followed other customers...

EVIL STUFF

...into other rotten stores...

BULLY SUPPLIES

...And Pulled their pants down, too!!!

mean machines

TRIPLE FLiP-O-RAMAS

animate the action cheesily. Here's How:

Hold Book open Like this...

Flip Page Back and Forth.

add your own sound effects!

Left hand here.

what
goes
up...

... must
come
down

... and
then
back
up
again.

Right
Thumb
here.

what
goes
up...

... must
come
down

... and
then
back
up
again.

ROBO CHIEF, Get in Here!!!

Yes, Mayor?

Go Find invisible Petey...

...And **DESTROY HiM!!!!!!!!!!**

Yes Sir!

ROBO CHIEF Ran to Town...

...and started a attack.

INVISIBLE Petey...

Prepare to meet thy Doom!

Invisible Petey was not afraid.

I ain't afraid!

Invisible Petey ran to a Rotten Store...

THE BAD

I'm Right over Here!

THE BAD GUYS

Oh, Yeah?

POW!

Invisible Petey ~~had~~ had zipped away just in time.

Tee hee!

He ran to another rotten store...

Haw! Haw!

EVIL BIKES

Hey, Robo Dude! I'm over here now!!!

OH Yeah?

POW

again, Petey zipped away just in time.

EVIL Bikes

zip

KA-BLAM

Invisible Petey Ran from ~~Rotten~~ Rotten Store...

Bad Goods

Yoo-Hoo!

BA-KLANG

...To Rotten Store.

Good Bads

Ya missed me!

LA-BEOUF

...Until every Rotten Store was gone.

Invisible ~~Petey~~ Petey ran to the playground.

Betcha can't catch me!

He ran over to the corkscrew slide...

I'm down here!

Oh Yeah?

POW!

SOON...

Ring Ring

HeLLo, Dr. Scum. Did RoBo chief Destroy Invisible PeTey?

Dr. Scum Told Mayor The bad news.

NOOOO

Mayor had one Last plan up her eviL sleeve.

She drove to the cop Station...

Mayor

COPS

DOG MAN!

YOU MUST STOP INVISIBLE PETEY!

USE YOUR DOG NOSE TO SNIFF HIM OUT.

GO GET HIM!

DOG MAN RAN TO TOWN.

SNIFF SNIFF SNIFF

Dog Man chased Invisible Petey all over Town...

CHOMP!

...but Invisible Petey was just too quick.

Haw Haw!

You'll never catch me, Dog Man...

...because I'm covered with invisible spray!

and I'm **NEVER** washing it off!!!!!

Then...

...Dog Man got a good idea.

DoG Man ran to a nearby Kiddie pool...

...and dived right in.

SPLASH

DoG Man was all weT.

Now it was time to dry off.

FLiP·O·RAMA

Left hand here.

Supa
Soaker

Right
Thumb
here.

Supa
Soaker

Now DOG Man could smell Petey And see him.

No---wait!

I can ~~see~~ exPLain!!!

Click!

Rats!!!

Soon... COP AWARDS

Ladies and gentlemen, Today we honor Dog Man...

...Because he Captured Petey and Stuff.

Get up here!

Speech!!!

Speech!!!

clap clap

Dog Man did not know how to give a speech...

...but he knew how to play a video!

Beep Beep

HOW is our evil Robot coming along?

Pretty good!

So Chief got his old job back...

and soon, every-thing was back to normal.

Hey!!!

CHAPTER 3

And now, get ready for a trip down memory Lane.

This next chapter is a comic we made back in first grade.

It's the extended director's cut!!

and I Fixed the Spelling!

Our teacher hated it so much, she sent this angry note to our moms.

Tee-hee!

we hope you Like it...

...better than she did!

Jerome Horwitz Elementary School

We put the "ow" in Knowledge

Dear Mr. and Mrs. Beard,

Once again I am writing to inform you of your son's disruptive activity in my classroom.

The assignment was to create a WRITTEN public service message to promote reading. Your son and his friend, Harold Hutchins (I am sending a nearly identical letter to Harold's mother), were specifically told NOT to make a comic book for this assignment.

As usual, they did exactly what they were told not to do (see attached comic book). When I confronted George about his disobedience, he claimed that this was not a comic book, but a "graphic novella." I am getting fed up with George's impudence.

I have told both boys on numerous occasions that the classroom is no place for creativity, yet they continue to make these obnoxious and offensive "comix." As you will see, this comic book contains multiple references to human and/or animal feces. It also features a very questionable scene of disregard for homeless/hungry individuals. There are scenes of smoking, violence, nudity, and don't get me started on the spelling and grammar. Frankly, I found the little trash bag "baby" at the end to be very disturbing. I mean, how is that even possible?!!?

George's silly, disruptive behavior, as well as these increasingly disgusting and scatological comic books, are turning my classroom into a zoo. I have spoken to Principal Krupp about Dog Man on numerous occasions. We both believe that you should consider psychological counseling for your son, or at the very least some kind of behavior modification drug to cure his "creative streak."

Regretfully,

Ms. Construde

Ms. Construde
Grade 1 Teacher

BOOK 'EM, DOG MAN

Tree House Comix

By George B. and Harold H.

One day Petey sat in his jail Cell feeling sad.

NEWS
DOG man wins again

Rats! Every time I have a evil Plan, DOG man always OUT-smarts me!

How Come He's SO Darn Smart ???

SO Petey De-Cided to Find Out!

CAT JAIL

So Long, suckas!

I'm Free!

NOW TO find OUT what makes DOG man so Smart!

SO PETEY sneaked TO DOG man's HOUSE.

hmm... He's reading!

PeteY used his smartometer to check...

DOGman was getting smarter by the minute.

So... Reading makes you smart, eh?

Then I must destroy all BOOKS!!!

one week Later...

Petey's Secret LAB

YOU reeka!

Petey zapped all the books in the city.

ZAP

BOOK STORE

HEY all our BOOKs are BLank!

BOOK STORE

Haw Haw

Then he zapped all the books in the country.

SCHOOL

Ours Too.

Ours Three

ZAP

PUBLIC LIBRARY

Then Petey got in a airplane and zapped all the books in the whole world!!!

TEE! HEE!

zap

now's my chance to have some fun...

Petey walked to the fancy car lot.

Hey, bub!!! Gimme a car!

Duh, my cat had eleven-teen puppies.

Okaaaay...

I'm just gonna take that one over there!

Duh, my mommy is five years old.

DOG man was pretty DUMB cuz he didn't Read no more...

But he Tried to Solve the crime anyway.

First he Questioned a chair...

Then he gAve a Lie detector Test to some pee...

He worked with a sketch artist...

And he even went on a steak-out.

Tim's Steak House

But he still couldn't solve the crime.

Tim's

Meanwhile, Petey was having trouble of his own...

He couldn't enjoy his new TV...

Break-ing News

'Cuz the shows were so Dumb!!!

Duh, welcome to the Thirteen o'clock News!!!

Then I took it out to the amusement park

GET OUT!

B-BUT we're in LOVE!

it was no Fun Being smarter than everybody else.

kick

Yeah, 12 Donuts PLEASE!

Sorry, we only sell them by the dozen.

O.K. ILL Take a dozen then.

Sorry, we don't have a dozen. We only have 16.

Fine! Gimme 16 Then!!!

Hey Buddy, can You help me???

I haven't eaten in three days. I'm Starving!!

Here. Have Some Bagels!

no Thanks. I don't Like Bagels.

I can't Take it anymore!

HEY, LOOK!

That's the Giraffe who gave us this cool car!!!

Oh yeah

Hey, Do you want a cigar?

sure!

zoom

BOOM

Petey's secret Lab

Petey started to get depressed.

He went to his secret Library...

Books
Keep out!

which contained the only Books Left on earth.

Petey Read and got smarter...

while the rest of the world got dumber...

Petey's Secret Lab

Duh, I just sold my Bike!

why?

and he hadn't had a bath in ages.

Boy, Did Petey stink!

Petey's secret Lab

meanwhile, Dog man was still trying to Find out who pooed in the chief's office.

His main suspect was a apple tree.

suddenly, Dog man smelled something...

DOG Man FOLLOWED the cat smell to Petey's hideout.

Petey's secret Lab

he went inside...

...and found Petey's secret Stash OF Books.

DOG man started to read...

DOG man Read all night Long...

...and GOT smarter and smarter.

The next morning, DOG man had a plan.

Petey's Secret LaB

He Brought PETEY'S BOOKS to The SCHOOL.

SCHOOL

and GaVe Them TO The kids.

The Kids read and Read.

and Then...

HOORAY!

We're smart again!

SOON, PETEY woke up...

...TO a shock!

MY BOOKS!

PETEY FOLLOWED the trail of BOOKS.

it Led to the school.

Then The RECESS BELL Rang!

OH, NO! I GOT to GeT those BOOKS!!!

FLIP-O-RAMAS

Left hand here.

the swing set
smacker

Right
Thumb
here.

The Swing Set
Smacker

OH NO! There's another Book By the SeeSaw!

FLIP·O·Rama

Left hand here.

The seesaw
smoosher

Right
Thumb
here.

The Seesaw
Smoosher

Left hand here.

SPRING
BREAK

Right
Thumb
here.

SPRING
BREAK

So Petey got captured...

Rats!

... Dog Man Reversed the Word-B-Gone 2000

And soon all the Books on earth got zapped Back to normal

zap

Hooray For Dog Man!!!

Trash

Trash

EPILOGUE

The next day, DOG man FOUND a security camera video.

They all watched it TOGether.

SUPA-SPY VIDEO

Soon They Discovered who pooed in the chief's office...

2:41

Tree House Comix Presents

Chief

CHAPTER 4

WEENIE WARS
THE FRANKS AWAKEN

DOG Man in
WEENIE WARS:
THE FRANKS awaken

One time at Cat Jail...

CAT JAIL

Mail delivery time!

Here, Fluffy, you got a Letter.

Thanks.

Here, Big Jim. You got candy.

Yay!

GUMMY MICE

BiG Jim

Meanwhile...

COPS

Hi, everybody!

I'm Back From Lunch!!!!

SPROING!

STOP it, DOG Man! stop!!!

LICK LICK

GET OFF!!!!

NOOOO!

CUT it OUT!!!

Remember--- Flip it,
Don't Rip it!!!!!!

Left
hand here.

WeLcome

Back,

Chief!

Right Thumb here.

WeLcome

Back,

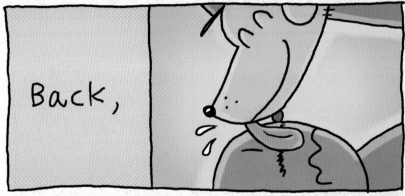

Chief!

BAD DOG MAN!!!

why do you always do that?

you just saw me, like, thirty minutes ago!!!

I HOPE you weren't LYing on my new COUCH!!!!!!

chief's office

Hmmm...

COOL...

...COOL...

HAW HAW HAW!

With this ~~whistle~~ DOG Whistle and this megaphone..

I can round up all the dogs in Town!

SWEE

Soon, every Dog in Town came running.

SWEE

Big Dogs...

SWee

...Little Dogs...

eeeee

The Poodle from the pet shop...

SWeee

Zuzu! come back!

Pene-Lope's Pets

Even Dog Man was not immune!

SWee

SWee

180

The weenies followed their evil leader out of cat jail...

... and into town.

Alright, weenies, time to take over!

And so, the Weenie war had begun.

umm...

what the???

we interrupt this comic for breaking news!

I'm sarah Hatoff with our top story.

Petey, the world's most evilest cat, has captured all dogs in the city!!!

That's Right! They're all locked inside this cage!

what do you plan to do with them?

watch and learn, sister!

Tee Hee !!!!

click

Behold, the Mutt-Masher 2000!!!

RRRRRRRR

OH, NO! The pointy teeth thingies are moving down!

Soon, those dogs will be crushed!

No way! Dog Man will save them!!!

nuh-uh! Dog man is **in** the cage!!!

chief

It was True! DoG Man was TRapped...

...and all his human Strength didn't help.

OH, NO!!! DoG Man is doomed!

why was I so mean to him???

There, there, Chief.

DoG Man will Save the day! You'll See!

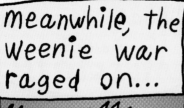

meanwhile, the weenie war raged on...

...It looked like the end was near...

...but it wasn't.

awww... Look!

how cute!

Say "cheese"!

click

Hey! That one made a little campfire!

Oh, how precious!

Soon, Philly came to life.

ME-
an-
wh-
iL-
e...

DOG Man Tried To stop
the crushing Pointy thingies...

...but his human strength
was giving out.

Oh, the
caninity!!!!

How could things
get any worse?

OH Look! Little baby hot dogs are starting a revolution!!!!

we're **not** Little babies! we're regular sized!

oh, how cute!

Grrrr!

we're not cute, either! we're **GANGSTA!**

awww! That one started a adorable Little fire!

That's **NOT** a adorable Little Fire!!! That's a *raging inFerno* OF DEATH!!!

What do I have to do To get a LitLle Respect around here?

DO I have TO DeSTROY EveryThing?

SuddenLy, inside The Mutt-Masher 2000, DOG Man got a great idea!

He reached into his shirt...

...and pulled out a bone!!!

Toss!

KLUNK

HEY!

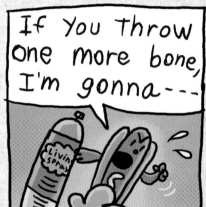

ALL the dogs were now safe...

...except **ONE!**

WELL, WELL, WELL...

PeTey FLew one way...

...and Dog Man FLew the other...

...and all that was Left was a bunch of Little baby hot dogs.

We're **NOT** LittLe babies!

We're Regular **SIZED!**

Yeah!

we may have Lost our Leader...

...and our giant gyro man...

Hip!

Hip!

Hooray!!!

Right Thumb here.

Hip!

Hip!

Hooray!!!

ain't you glad chief ain't mad at DOG Man no more?

I sure amn't!

HOORAY FOR DOG MAN!

REFOCUS FORM

~~REDO~~

Name: Harold H.

Grade: 1-C

Teacher: Mr. Constitude

I engaged in unacceptable behavior
by: # making copies of
dog man comix in
office.

My behavior caused other students and teachers to
feel: Freak out

How will my behavior change in the future? be
more quieter when
making copies of dog man
comix in office.

I am ready to re-join the classroom. Yes ___ No X
Why? too busy making
dog man comix

Student signature: Harold H.

~~NO DRAWING~~

HOW MANY TIMES
DO WE HAVE TO
TALK About This ???

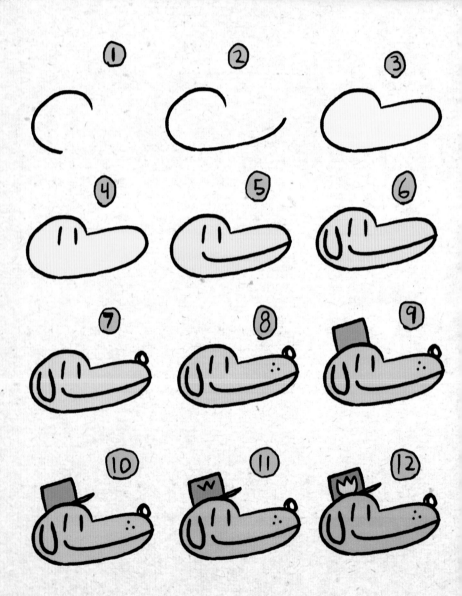

BE EXPRESSIVE!!!

Happy

Happier

Supa Happy

Worried

Sad

Determined

ascared

Angry

Sleepy

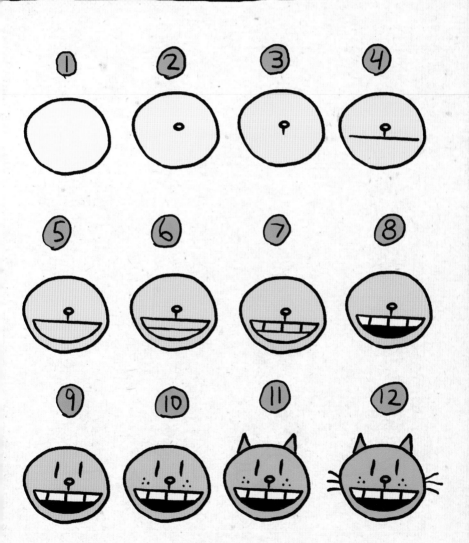

BE EXPRESSIVE

evil

Diabolical

Supa Sinister

Sad

Angry

Supa angry

Supa, supa angry

Surprised

Sleepy

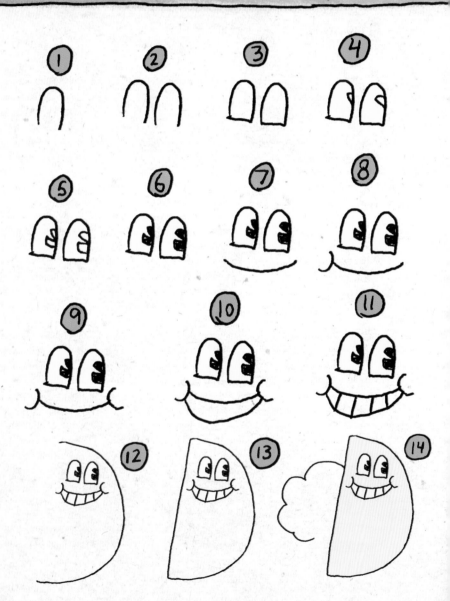

BE EXPRESSIVE!!!

Mad

Surprised

Content

Grossed-
out

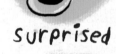

Ouch!

Steamed

afraid

Laughing

Sleepy

230

① ② ③ ④

⑤ ⑥ ⑦ ⑧

BE EXPRESSIVE!!!

Happy   angry   sad   obsequious

ABOUT THE AUTHOR-ILLUSTRATOR

When Dav Pilkey was a kid, he suffered from ADHD, dyslexia, and behavioral problems. Dav was so disruptive in class that his teachers made him sit out in the hall every day. Luckily, Dav loved to draw and make up stories. He spent his time in the hallway creating his own original comic books.

In the second grade, Dav Pilkey created a comic book about a superhero named Captain Underpants. His teacher ripped it up and told him he couldn't spend the rest of his life making silly books.

Fortunately, Dav was not a very good listener.

ABOUT THE COLORIST

Jose Garibaldi grew up on the South Side of Chicago. As a kid, he was a daydreamer and a doodler, and now it's his full-time job to do both. Jose is a professional illustrator, painter, and cartoonist who has created work for Dark Horse Comics, Disney, Nickelodeon, MAD Magazine, and many more. He lives in Los Angeles, California, with his wife and their cats.

DOG MAN 2
UNLEASHED

From George and Harold

CALLING ALL CARS!

A Brand-New DOG Man Novel is COMING SOON!

In a Time of darkness and despair...

When strange new villains arise...

...and sinister scoundrels Poison the minds of the meek...

We Love You, PeteY!

Yeah!

Hubba-Hubba!

Only one Dog-headed cop can save the day!

DOG Man, the City is under attacks!

who wants to save the day?

Who's a good hero?

who wants to stop the bad guys?

Go get 'em!!!!

YOU'LL HOWL WITH Laughter.

You'll SCRATCH WITH SUSPENSE!

YOU'LL Scoot your butt on the carpet with JOY!

RIGHT THUMB here

You'll Howl with Laughter.

You'll Scratch with Suspense!

You'll Scoot your butt on the carpet with Joy!